THE GIFT OF THORNS

THORNS

STUDY GUIDE

T0308412

THE GIFT OF THORNS

Jesus, the Flesh, and the War for Our Wants

A. J. SWOBODA

HarperChristian
Resources

ZONDERVAN REFLECTIVE

The Gift of Thorns Study Guide
Copyright © 2024 by A. J. Swoboda

Published in Grand Rapids, Michigan, by Zondervan. Zondervan is a registered trademark of The Zondervan Corporation, L.L.C., a wholly owned subsidiary of HarperCollins Christian Publishing, Inc.

Requests for information should be addressed to customercare@harpercollins.com.

Zondervan titles may be purchased in bulk for educational, business, fundraising, or sales promotional use. For information, please email SpecialMarkets@Zondervan.com.

ISBN 978-0-310-15332-0 (softcover)
ISBN 978-0-310-15333-7 (ebook)

Published in association with literary agent Tawny Johnson of Illuminate Literary Agency, www.illuminateliterary.com.

Cover design: Spencer Fuller, Faceout Studio
Cover photos: Shutterstock; GettyImages
Interior design: Kait Lamphere

Printed in the United States of America

23 24 25 26 27 28 29 30 31 32 33 34 35 /TRM/ 17 16 15 14 13 12 11 10 9 8 7 6 5 4 3 2 1

CONTENTS

INTRODUCTION

We have quite the journey ahead of us.

If you've never taken time to take a look at your own desires or what the Bible says about them, then put on your seat belt. You're in for a ride. What you hold in your hand is a study guide intended to accompany both my book *The Gift of Thorns* and the video sessions that correspond with it. The three are shaped to go alongside each other. In this guide, you'll be led through some of the main concepts and ideas that I flesh out in my book, which asks, "How are we formed into godliness in our human desire?" More than anything, this project is a biblical, theological, and experiential exploration into one of the things that makes us human: our God-given desire. Not only will we take time to explore our own desires, but we will also traverse a basic understanding of what the Bible says about God's desire, what has happened to our desires, and how desires are transformed when we choose to follow Jesus and be open to the Holy Spirit. A trigger warning: Along the way, you will be asked to look at the sensitive parts of your heart that we tend to ignore. We won't keep things shallow. We will "go there."

Knowing where we are going may be helpful. Each session included here has four parts. The first section, "Introduction," orients you to the main concept or idea of the corresponding chapter and video session. It will include some food for thought intended to parallel what you encounter in the video. It would be wise to watch the video before engaging the study guide material. The second section, "Discussion," is intended for group discussion in the chance that you are undertaking this journey with a small group, friends, family, or church. I *highly* recommend going on this journey with others. Next, the "Reflection Questions" offer unique opportunities for individual reflection on the content that has been presented. A final "Closing" section will sum things up, offering a sneak peek of what is to come in the next session. Good news: this same rhythm can be expected in each of the eleven sessions provided in this study guide. I strongly urge you not only to read the book *The Gift of Thorns* along with this study, but also to come to this discussion with a Bible in hand.

We all have busy lives, so this study guide is intended to provide you freedom to take each step through these sessions at your own pace. I encourage going slowly. If you're the group leader for this study guide discussion, be sure to take ample time for the discussion section. Don't rush the conversation sparked by the sessions. The discussion questions are intended to spark intimate and important conversation about the nature of our own desires. We shouldn't rush this process.

We begin. Even as I write this, I offer a prayer on your behalf:

In the name of the Father, the Son, and the Holy Spirit, would you find grace and mercy along the way as you walk through what I submit to you here.

It is an honor to walk with you a little through what has been a remarkable journey for me. I hope it will be a helpful one for you as well.

A. J. Swoboda, PhD
Lent 2023 | Eugene, OR

GOD'S DESIRE

Introduction

Ours is a world bathed in desire.

Nothing exists accidentally. Everything—literally everything—is a result of some kind of design, purpose, or desire. Wherever you find yourself, look around you right now. You will likely observe a variety of items: tables, trees, books, coffee cups, couches, a fireplace, even a table upon which one could write. These things didn't just come out of thin air. Each thing you see is the result of someone's desire.

To exist is to be *wanted*.

God did not have to create. He was not compelled or forced to undertake the action of creating everything. God created for one reason: he desired to. Even the creation story of the Bible is possible because God—who stands outside of time—*wanted* to create out of sheer love. God's desire brought everything into existence. When we look at the beginning of the creation story in Genesis 1 and 2, we are told of a God who speaks light into being, sends solar systems into their spinning, and gives the land, plants, and birds all their sacred place in the world. Over all of it, time and again, God declares each and every creation to be "good . . . good . . . good" (Gen. 1:4, 10, 12).

Still, *why* would God create?

This is why the Bible offers such a compelling account: it gives us an origin story for everything. Origin stories are all the rage right now. In recent years, Hollywood has become enamored with stories that narrate the background accounts of some of our favorite heroes, from Luke Skywalker to Batman. Why? Because everything is the way it is, in part, because of where it comes from. In a sense, then, we can see the early chapters of Genesis as a kind of origin story going all the way back to "In the beginning" (Gen. 1:1). And when we look carefully, this origin story has remarkable explanatory power.

We begin with a God creating through his word, but we are left wondering: What happened *before* the beginning? What was God doing before he decided to make everything we can see? The early chapters of Genesis do not explicitly answer how the origin story had its origin. But we get a clue later on in the writings of the New Testament. While we're not told the particular activities of God before the creation event, we are told about the nature of God who created everything. "God is love," the apostle John tells us (1 John 4:8). This, for theologians, is a critical description of God's being because it tells us not what God does but *who* God is. Yes, God loves. God loves each and every one of us. But more than that, God *is* love. That is to say, his essence, being, and nature are as a God who is love.

In some way, this helps explain *why* God created. For ages, theologians have long repeated the maxim that God created the world "out of nothing" (or *ex nihilo* in Latin). I affirm the basic impulse of the doctrine that God did, indeed, create out of nothing rather than reorganizing existing matter. But I'm tempted to suggest this particular doctrine remains a tad unsatisfying. Why? Because, in a sense, God created out of something—not preexisting matter, but love and desire. Before creation was, creation was wanted. In the iconic words of Charles Spurgeon, before it was made, "the great universe lay in the mind of God like unborn forests in the acorn's cup."[1] The very conception of creation did not come from nowhere. It came from the mind, the heart, the desire of the Creator. Indeed, it was desire that gave birth to every last nook and cranny of the cosmos.

Most conversations about creation in Christian circles obsess almost exclusively over the "how" of creation—for example, how old the earth is. These are important, fascinating, and pressing conversations. But more pertinent for a conversation about desire is the "why" of creation. As Auguste Comte famously posited in 1835, we'll never find out what the stars are made out of. His point? We can study the stars, but we can't study *why* the stars. This has been called The Question by many scientists. For while scientific inquiry can help us see what exists, it can't, with much explanatory power, explain why it exists. Science, able to explain the stars' existence, can't explain the reason for their very existence.[2]

---

1. Quoted in Haddon Robinson, *Biblical Sermons: How Twelve Preachers Apply the Principles of Biblical Preaching* (Grand Rapids: Baker, 1997), 196.
2. Although some attempts have been made. See, for example, Lawrence M. Krauss, *A Universe from Nothing: Why There Is Something Rather Than Nothing* (New York: Atria, 2012).

As did Comte, some have attempted a guess or two. Some of these guesses are quite comical. For instance, science novelist John Updike suggested that if there was indeed a God, he most certainly decided to create the whole cosmos out of boredom. John Horgan, author of *The End of Science* and *Rational Mysticism*, was struck by his own epiphany:

> If there is a God, He created this heart-breaking world because He was suffering from a cosmic identity crisis, triggered by His own confrontation with The Question. . . . God is as mystified as we are by existence.[3]

The Bible has a unique perspective on why God created. And it has to do, in part, with what God was doing before he created the world. Truth be told, we don't know what God was doing before creation. But we know who God was before he created. God was, is, and always will be love. This is God's nature. It is a compelling thing to consider that God's love for us as his creatures is not dependent on our even existing. God loved us before "us" even existed! Before creation, before making, before spinning the galaxy into its being, God was love.

God made the world because God is love. It is out of this love that God desired everything to be. One of my favorite ways to describe this is that God created the garden of Eden out of sheer delight of desire. God did not create compulsively because he had to. Rather, God created because he desired to. God did not create a garden because God needed more vegetables. God, who is love, simply desired to create. Michael Reeves, a theologian, reflects on this very mystery in his book *Delighting in the Trinity*:

> A father is someone who gives life, who "begets" children. . . . If before all things, God was eternally a father, that means "God" is an inherently outgoing, others-centered, life-giving God. The Christian God did not give life for the first time when he decided to create the universe. We're asked to consider that from eternity God in his essence is life-giving.[4]

---

3. John Horgan, "Science Will Never Explain Why There's Something Rather Than Nothing," *Cross-Check*, April 23, 2012, https://blogs.scientificamerican.com/cross-check/science-will-never-explain-why-theres-something-rather-than-nothing/.

4. Michael Reeves, *Delighting in the Trinity: An Introduction to the Christian Faith* (Downers Grove, IL: IVP, 2012), 24. I'm grateful to my friend Tim Mackie who pointed out this fabulous text to me. I'll never be the same.

Remarkable as it may sound, even if we didn't exist, God would still be love. In the first session, we explore this mystery at length and consider that everything in the entire world and creation is an overflow of this God of love.

Discussion

To fully understand ourselves as humans—humans with desire—we first must see God as a God of desire. As we will soon see, it is impossible to separate our own human desires from God's desire. But we need to begin by focusing on God's desires primarily. With this topic in mind, reflect on the following.

1 We usually think about human desire, but we often overlook the idea of God as a being who desires. If you have never considered it, why do you think you haven't? If you have, what are some of the thoughts that came to you about God's desire?

2 Does the idea that God created out of desire make you uncomfortable? Or does it bring you a sense of comfort? Explain why or why not.

3 The idea that "God is love" is a transformational concept. It speaks to the nature of God. How is your sense of self affected when you consider the fact that God would be love even if you did not exist? How does this truth impact your self-understanding?

4 Do you feel wanted by God? If so, what does that feel like? If not, what does that feel like?

5 Do you agree with the assessment that everything exists because it is wanted and desired by God? Explain your response.

Reflection Questions

1 What do you think about this simple premise that "God is love" (1 John 4:8) as it relates to God's creation? Do you believe this accounts for *why* God made everything? Or do you think there is more to it than that? Explain.

2 Part of the grounding of our own existence as human beings is that we were desired by God. Some of us may feel undesired or unwanted. Does the idea that God wanted you into existence change the way you understand God or yourself?

3 Reflect on a time in your life when you felt unwanted. How does the idea of God creating out of his unending love change the way you think about that time?

4 In this session Swoboda tells the story of the "Rainbow Bench." This story gets at the heart of the gospel message—not only were we made by God, but we are wanted by God. How, in your mind, does the gospel overlap with God's desire?

5 Swoboda talks about one of the main questions he gets from his students: "Why would God create the world knowing how bad it would become?" Indeed, the world we find ourselves in is not going the way God wanted it to go. Things are out of whack. What do you think of his response to the question? Does it help us understand why God would want a world even in its broken state?

6 Do you believe God wants a world of sin, injustice, and evil as we are experiencing it now?

7 In light of your response to the previous question, would you say the God of the Bible always gets what he wants? Explain.

8 One of the main ways we determine our own desires is by understanding the things with which we are disappointed. Disappointment, above all, speaks to our desires. Do you believe God is disappointed with you? Why? Why not?

9 Throughout, we have considered that the God of the Bible is a God of desire. In what ways do you believe God's desire is the same as ours? And in what ways do you think God's desires are different from our own?

10 Paul writes that God "wants all people to be saved and to come to a knowledge of the truth" (1 Tim. 2:4). What do you make of this? What is Paul trying to communicate about God's desire?

11 Sin is a major theme throughout the biblical narrative. In light of what we've discussed, do you think it's fair to say that sin could be defined as whenever God's desire is not lived out by humans? Explain your response.

Closing

We have explored some of the core biblical literature around the God of the Bible as a God of desire. We have made the case that God created everything because God is a God of desire who is love. As we move forward, let us rejoice in the simple knowledge that the God of the universe is the same God who pursues us in Jesus. God made us out of desire. And it is his desire to know and walk with us today. In our next session, we will begin to zoom in on our own human desires. Indeed, our desires have been corrupted. But long before they were corrupted, our desires were "good" with the rest of creation.

HUMAN DESIRE

Introduction

In our previous session, we explored the foundational idea that God created the world out of desire because God's nature is to love. Quite simply, "God is love" (1 John 4:8). This is an enormously important part of who we are as creatures. One could say God's desire for us is an inherent part of who we are as beings made by a God of desire. "Humankind's greatness rests solely on the fact that God in his incomprehensible goodness has bestowed his love upon him," wrote German theologian Helmut Thielicke. "God does not love us because we are so valuable; we are valuable because God loves us."[1] The value inherent in a human transcends their temporal existence. Our value is grounded in God—in the very desire of God. We *are* because God is love. No more. No less. Our identity as sons and daughters of God rests more than anything on the fact that God desires us. Our entire identity is shaped by being desired by God.

When God created humans, they bore a unique responsibility in the garden God had made. The humans, namely, were created in "the image of God" (Gen. 1:27). Something sets the humans apart from the rest of the created beasts. As we zoom in on the garden story of Genesis 1–2, we quickly observe that humans are extended an astonishing level of responsibility and authority in the garden environment God made. The humans are told to "rule" (Gen. 1:28) in the garden as God's representatives to cultivate,

---

1. Helmut Thielicke, *Nihilism: Its Origin and Nature, with a Christian Answer,* trans. John W. Doberstein (London: Routledge and Kegan Paul, 1962), 110.

care, and "take care of" (Gen. 2:15) the garden God planted. God, as the Creator, gives these humans remarkable authority to care for—and potentially subvert—God's good world. Yes, they are given authority to do good. But, as we soon discover, they are also given freedom to do great evil. Sadly, the story of the human race is marked by their decision to choose the ways of the serpent and self over the words of God who walks among them. But humans weren't created as corrupted beings. Humans were created "good."

Interestingly, the fact that God gives authority to humans gives us a clearer understanding of God's nature. The God of the Bible is a power-sharing God. That is to say that God bestows upon the humans his authority to either rule well or rule wrong.

Years ago, a Christian thinker named Simone Weil spoke of this act of creation as God's "renunciation." That is, by creating humans, God limits himself. God is creating another power and refusing to rule alone. Reflecting on Weil's thought, Christian philosopher Diogenes Allen draws the parallel of a human author of a book. He uses the illustration of the Christian author Dorothy Sayers. When authors like Sayers choose to write the story of some character, Allen suggests, they do so making room for their character to become themselves:

> Writers must restrain their own personalities to create a personality which is not their own. In order that something may exist beyond and apart from themselves, they are required to renounce themselves. Good literature is no mere extension of a writer's personality, but entails an ethical act of self-renunciation so that something else might exist.[2]

Allen suggests that God is not only giving human beings life in the garden of Eden, but is simultaneously practicing an act of self-limitation by allowing someone else's desire and will to exist in the garden. God is willingly divesting himself of the right to total and universal control over the universe. God is sharing power. "When God creates," Allen finishes, "it means that he allows something to exist which is not himself. This requires an act of profound renunciation."[3] God is a God of desire. But God also gives his creatures desire.

---

2. Diogenes Allen, *Traces of God* (New York: Seabury, 2006), 35.
3. Allen, *Traces of God*, 35.

Made in the image of God, the humans are given good and godly desires as they hold authority in the garden. As you'll recall, in this session I discuss "original desire," the hardwired desires God created humans with in the garden of Eden. One of these original desires is the desire for intimacy and relationship with other humans. The order of the creation reveals that the man was created first. We are not told for how long, but we know it was long enough to experience what the text calls "aloneness" (see Gen. 2:18). God did not create the man to be alone. That is to say, the first man was not created with all of his needs immediately provided for. He still longed for someone other than God.

Humans were made to experience longing. Adam experienced this. In fact, when we compare God's creation of humans to that of the animals, we see one distinct difference. The animals are created two by two, in pairs of male and female. Humans, too, were created male and female, but they were not both created at the same exact time. They were created at different moments, not as in an immediate pair. God took his time to create the woman after the man had been made.

Why would God create the first man with a built-in experience of aloneness? In his book *Man in History*, theologian Hans Urs von Balthasar suggests this delay is a paradigm for understanding the way God works in the world and in our hearts. Balthasar writes,

> Even Adam, according to the legend of Paradise, although created in the fullness of God's grace, had an unsatisfied longing until God had given him Eve. Adam transcended and sought through the whole of nature—naming and hence knowing—looking for that which would bring him fulfillment and completion. He did not find it. It is strange that human nature, obviously quite different from the animals which were already created two by two, has to *long* for the other.[4]

We are, unlike any of the other animals, created with a desire for relational intimacy with God and each other. This is an original desire. It is the hardwired desire that God made humans with. He did not create us with desires that are bad. Nor with desires that lead us astray. A good Creator instilled good desires in us at the moment of our invention.

---

4. Hans Urs von Balthasar, *Man in History: A Theological Study* (London: Sheed and Ward, 1968), 84–85, emphasis added.

Now, in future sessions we will look at how our desires have been inescapably corrupted by what we will call sin. But we mustn't jump over Genesis 1–2 too quickly. Our desires were good before they were corrupted. You can probably name some of these good, original desires that have been divinely orchestrated. The desire for relationship—that deep, insatiable hunger we have for connection and interpersonal revelation. The desire for friendship—the need for companionship. The desire for food—don't forget that God instructed the man and the woman to "eat" from any (save one) tree in the garden of Eden. The desire for sex—one of the first commands was for humans to "be fruitful and increase in number" (Gen. 1:28). No doubt he matched the call with the glorious desire that would fulfill it.

Sure, we are people with broken desires. But underneath the debris of our fractured longings exists a glorious terrain of designed desire made by the hand of God.

Discussion

Too often, Christians have a low view of desire, believing it to always be wrong, bad, or corrupted. But we can't begin with a negative view of desire because that is not our original creation. We must begin, first, by understanding desire as it was originally intended. With this in mind, take some time to reflect on the following questions.

1 For many Christians, the conversation about desire immediately turns toward corrupted desire. Desire, it is assumed, is always a bad thing. Do you believe this assumption matches what we see in the early chapters of Genesis? Explain.

2 As you think about your own desires, name the parts of your desire you have believed were bad that perhaps God calls good. Have you been kind to yourself for having the desire that God created?

3 Should we have a more balanced understanding of desire? And if so, how can we more faithfully appropriate the positive vision of desire the Bible begins with?

4 In your experience, would you say Christianity has a reputation of being anti-desire? Why or why not?

5 As you think about Christian faith, why do you believe that some have taken on a critical or negative perspective toward desire?

Reflection Questions

1 We tend to be deeply formed by what we have been taught. What, if any, Christian teaching on the topic of desire have you ever experienced or heard? What core ideas have been most formative in your understanding of human desire?

2 What are your immediate, gut-level responses to the idea presented in this session that humans were created to need relationships with people—or that they were made to "need more than God"? Do you believe this is true? Or is this an overstatement?

3 As you reflect on the discussion of Adam's creation, what do you think God might have had in mind by creating the man first and giving him the experience of aloneness before the creation of the woman?

4 Do you find yourself to be a person driven by longing? How so? And where does that longing come from?

5 Humans, we found, are made in the "image of God." Swoboda argues that part of this image is a unique human capacity for longing. God is a desiring God. And humans reflect this. What else is part of the "image of God" that humans have?

6 God opts to create a world of humans with desire. God did not create a world of robots that do not desire and want. What do you make of the fact that God does not desire to be the only being that desires?

7 Why do you think we tend to overemphasize the sinfulness of desire rather than the way desire was meant to be?

8 Take a moment to reflect on a desire you experience that you believe to be against God's design and plan. Now consider if perhaps underneath this desire is an original, good desire that has simply become twisted or contorted.

9 Given how central desire is to the human experience from the time of our creation, do you believe enough attention is given to the topic of desire in the teaching and preaching of the church? Why? Why not?

10 Have you ever had a Christian leader or friend affirm a desire within you? What was that experience like? Did it help you? Or harm you?

11 Do you—or do you not—take time to sit and reflect on the actual desires of your heart? If so, how? If not, why?

12 Why might it be important to take necessary space and time in your life to explore the desires of your heart? Does any fruit come from listening to those desires? Or is it simply a distraction from your Christian walk?

Closing

Indeed, desire was created good. But it was soon devastated by what we discuss in the next chapter. The next session shows how desire spirals out of control following the fall of humanity and their disobedience to God's commands in Genesis 1–2. Things get painful from Genesis 3 on. But still, we must constantly remind ourselves that before things got bad, they were so, so "good." The goodness of our desire matters. And taking time to appreciate the way God made us paves the way for us to experience the healing of our desires. We won't change the things we hate. But we can change the things we love.

SATAN'S DESIRE

Introduction

In the video for this session, we took time to unpack what for many of us may be a new perspective on the person and work of evil. That is, we looked at the particular desires of Satan. Part of our exploration up to this point has been an in-depth examination of the first three chapters of the Bible. As we consider those early chapters, it might be helpful to think of them as a kind of two-act play. Genesis 1 and 2 (or Act 1) tell about God's creation and the way God wanted things to be. Then Genesis 3 (or Act 2) continues the story by narrating how creation became subverted into a cosmic rebellion by a serpent desiring its ruin. When read together, these two acts serve as a stark contrast—almost like "before and after" photos. They show us that desire existed before the cosmic rebellion and how human desire became distorted by the fall.

One of the key means by which the serpent acts is by manipulating the good desires of the humans, by insinuating that they are "missing out" on something they could have had. "When you eat . . . you will be like God" (Gen. 3:5). Satan goes out of his way to convince the humans that they could become like God. Of course, in so doing, he intentionally neglects to mention that the humans were already created in the "image of God." One of the most dangerous operating principles of Satan is that he wants the first humans—and us—to feel isolated, forgotten, and not nurtured or cared for. This is at the core of his desire for each of our lives.

Another way the serpent works is by tempting us to desire things that have a quality of beauty but, in the end, aren't for us. Take, for example, the "tree of knowledge of good and evil" (Gen 2:17). We are told it is a beautiful tree and "pleasing to the eye" (Gen. 3:6), yet this is the one tree humans are not to eat from. This point is important because it reveals that just because something is beautiful doesn't mean that it's for us. The enemy often tempts us with beautiful and glorious things. We assume sin is dark. But we learn something else here. Sin can have the quality of beauty. The fruit was pleasing to the eye.

The experience of missing out is a critical one throughout the Bible. Perhaps you've heard of a character in the New Testament Gospels known as Thomas. Sadly, in the history of the church, he has been called "Doubting Thomas," a name not given to him in the actual literature of the gospels. Thomas undergoes a series of existential crises around the resurrection of Jesus.[1] Thomas "was not with the disciples when Jesus came" (John 20:24). He believes he has fully missed out. In his apparent frustration, Thomas tells the other disciples, "Unless I see the nail marks in his hands and put my finger where the nails were, and put my hand into his side, I will not believe" (John 20:25).

We are in a vulnerable place when we believe the lie that we have entirely missed out. For Thomas, it was in missing out on seeing the resurrected Jesus for the first time that he became susceptible to doubt. For many of us, we become most susceptible to temptation when we feel like everyone else is enjoying life and we are not. When everyone else is able to get their dreams fulfilled and we can't. When everyone else has a great marriage. When everyone else is having a blessed existence. Much like the author of Psalm 73, we may ask God why the wicked are "always free of care" and "go on amassing wealth" (v. 12). For many, we need to slow down and pay close attention to our hearts when we think everyone else has "it," and we are missing out.

We are told that the thief comes to "steal and kill and destroy" (John 10:10). He is seeking to undo the works of God. The prophet Isaiah describes the king of Babylon this way:

> You said in your heart,
> "I will ascend to the heavens;
> I will raise my throne
> above the stars of God;
> I will sit enthroned on the mount of assembly,

---

1. A. J. Swoboda, *After Doubt: How to Question Your Faith without Losing It* (Grand Rapids: Brazos, 2020).

on the utmost heights of Mount Zaphon.
I will ascend above the tops of the clouds;
I will make myself like the Most High." (Isa. 14:13–14)

Throughout Christian history, this passage has been interpreted as language God also speaks against Satan. Notice the word "ascend." In pride, Satan wants to take God's place, to undo the works of God. But Satan can only mimic the works of God. For although Satan wanted to ascend to the throne of God, God descended from his throne to love humanity. Ours is a world marked more by Satan's desires than by God's desires. We try to ascend to godhood while God descends to manhood. No wonder we keep missing each other.

The desires of Satan are real. It is sobering to consider that the enemy of our souls has desires *for* us. The enemy desires us to exist in constant sin, trapped by our evil desires and impulses. The enemy wants us to live in a constant torrent of discouragement, disparagement, and hopelessness. The enemy wants us to experience waves of despair and isolation. It is critical that followers of Jesus wake up to the desires our enemy has for us. For only in doing so can we withstand them. We confront the desires of our enemy by understanding and desiring the desires of God. This is what life often feels like: being torn between the desires of God and the desires of God's enemy.

God's desires. Or Satan's desires. Most children learn early on that two parents can have different desires. Some parents are "yes" parents. And some are "no" parents. Kids have to learn whom to go to. Many learn, with two parents who have two desires, it is wise to gravitate toward one to get what is wanted.

In a way, we all learn to gravitate toward the desires of the one who gives us what we want. God is most interested in our formation into the image of Christ—not in giving us everything we want. Satan, on the other hand, has far less noble desires. He does not wish to see us formed into the image of Christ. Rather, Satan offers us what we want so we will become enslaved to his kingdom, ways, and desires. God calls us to a holy life. And as a result, he often gives us a divine "no" to our wants. Like any child, we are tempted to go to the authority that always gives us what we want.

But we must resist this temptation. We must learn to come in faith to the God of the universe who has our best interests in mind. In the end, that is what the Christian journey is all about. We are called not to "gain the whole world" (Matt. 16:26) but to exhibit a steadfast love and fidelity to God above all things.

Discussion

Most Christians do not have a well-developed understanding of the desires of the evil one. In fact, too often we blithely ignore the powers of darkness and underestimate their influence in the world and in our lives. Understanding the methods of Satan is a critical part of our own formation. In light of this truth, take time to discuss the following questions.

1 Have you ever thought about or considered what Satan *wants* to do? Why is he doing what he does? What is his motivation?

2 Is spending time thinking through the desires of the devil important for our own Christian maturity? Why or why not? Is it merely a distraction from more important conversations?

3 In your discussion, tell a story of a time when you were tempted to listen more to the desires of Satan than to the desires of God. What happened?

4 As you think about the ways the enemy has caused disruption in your own Christian formation, what have you noticed? What does it appear the enemy of your soul wants you to do?

5 How do you believe one can discern (or critically understand) the difference between the desires of the devil and the desires of God? What are ways we can carefully know the difference between the two?

Reflection Questions

1 Swoboda talks about Paul's idea of *methodia*—or the "methods" of the evil one. Think for a few moments about times in your life when you have experienced temptation. What do those experiences share in common?

2 Swoboda talks about Satan as a "groomer" who knows what we need. No doubt, the serpent deceived the man and the woman by weaponizing their desire. How, in your experience, have you seen your own good and godly desires weaponized against you?

3 Think of a time when you were able to recognize and stand firm against the methods of the enemy.

4 As the video for this session discusses, there is an important connection in the Bible between "seeing" and "taking." Can you sum up this basic idea in your own words? How does Scripture connect these two ideas?

5 Can you tell of a moment in your life when you "saw" something you wanted and "took" it for yourself and afterward realized you had taken something God never wanted you to have? What did you learn from that experience?

6 We also looked at how Jesus, in the Last Supper, upends the "seeing" and "taking" by providing for humans a meal. How do you think Jesus meets us in our proclivity toward "seeing" and "taking"?

7 The video for this session talks about how the "mother tongue of the evil one is insinuation." Do you believe this is true? Why or why not?

8 As you think about yourself and your own experience, what areas of your life have you found most prone to having your desires used against you for the wrong purposes?

9 The video discusses how Jesus faced his own temptation in the wilderness narrative. What do you believe is the most important part of that account for us today?

10 What can we learn from the way Jesus faced the devil in his own temptation? How can we model our lives after the example he set?

11 This session connects the story of the garden of Eden to that of the wilderness narrative. What is the basic connection between these two accounts? And what can we learn by reading them in light of each other?

12 What practices can we begin to embody that will help us hear the voice of God over the voice of the evil one?

Closing

As we have now taken time to look at the desires of Satan, we are next going to explore how Genesis 3 impacts all of us. We are going to look at our "flesh" as the place where the desires of the unregenerate person continue to live. We have focused on the evil one here. But we must remember—in the words of the author of Hebrews—to "fix [our] thoughts on Jesus" (Heb. 3:1). The goal here is not to take our eyes off the one we worship. Rather, it is to have a better understanding of the desires and methods of the one who wants to keep us from looking at Jesus.

FLESHLY DESIRE

Introduction

In this session we explore the topic of the "flesh." As I note in the book and in the video sessions, the flesh is that place in our lives where Satan seeks to appeal to our desires. It is there, in our broken, sinful state, that our desires are weaponized against us. In our flesh, we face our greatest temptations, fall with regularity, and are enticed to live in ways that are contrary to the way of Jesus.

We ultimately end up growing whatever we feed the most. That is to say, we become more and more like either the Spirit or the flesh within us. A friend of mine who is writing on the topic of theology and social media is keen to say to the students at our university, "We become whatever we like."[1] If we sow into the Spirit, we will reap from the Spirit. But if we sow into the flesh, we will reap more flesh (see Gal. 6:8). This is what the desires of the flesh and the desires of the Spirit share in common: the more we follow them, the more we *want* them. In this way, the laws of spiritual things and physical things are quite different. In the physical, we are satiated when we eat. But in the spiritual, when we feed on the desires of the flesh or the Spirit, we hunger *more* for the desires of the flesh or the Spirit. As Jesus said, "Flesh gives birth to flesh, but the Spirit gives birth to spirit" (John 3:6).

We become what we give ourselves to. Put another way, we form a new attachment

---

1. Thanks to Josh Little, professor of formation and Christian Scriptures at Bushnell University where I teach, for this clever wording and thinking.

to our flesh as we feed it. In recent years, attachment theory has become an increasingly important discipline in the psychological sciences that helps us understand the kind of healthy relationships humans need with their caregivers to flourish. Some of us had healthy attachments to our caregivers. And some of us did not. Much of the healing we will need to walk through later in life likely involves some of the unhealthy and unfulfilled attachments from our childhood. Jim Wilder is a clinical psychologist who has written on the power of sin. He argues that at the moment the man and the woman chose to listen to the serpent, a new kind of neural bond, or attachment, was formed between humans and this entity in the garden:

> Attachment love forms a kind of permanent "glue" uniting two people. The human brain is pre-wired to glue/attach itself to the source of its life. Thus, the one who feeds us, gives us our drink, or gives us shelter will become the center of our attachment love. Hebrew uses the word *dabiq* ("to glue") in commanding us to attach permanently to God (i.e. Deuteronomy 11:22). Letting the serpent feed us was an attachment mistake. Asking the Baals to feed us or provide fertility creates attachments to them. Those who feed on words of life, eat the Bread of Heaven, drink Living Water and dwell in the shelter of the Most High also build attachment love. The love that attaches us to the source of life is attachment love.[2]

Just as we formed an attachment to God as our caregiver, upon listening to the serpent, a new attachment was forged. And we are still paying the price. At that very moment, we traded in a nurturing, life-giving, and sustaining relationship with the God of the universe for a relationship with a fallen angelic being who cannot sustain us or provide for us.

This is the flesh. The flesh is the part of us that remains "attached" to the works of the enemy. And we all have it. As I say in this session, the flesh is not something that simply goes away the minute we begin to follow Jesus. In fact, we will walk with it until the day we are resurrected in the presence of Jesus. The flesh doesn't simply go away over time. Rather, we have to actively crucify it.

Many Christians live in a constant state of shame that they still have desires within

2. Jim Wilder, "Thinking with God: Weaving God's Thoughts into Human Identities and Relationships," Life Model Works, June 2020, https://lifemodelworks.org/wp-content/uploads/2021/06/Thinking-With-God-Spiritual-Formation-Wilder.pdf.

that are not of Jesus. Time and again, I find that my students have a cloud of shame hanging over their heads for continuing to experience temptations years after coming to faith in Christ. But this is not a crisis of sanctification. If anything, it is a crisis of theology. The presence of temptation—as evidenced in the story of Jesus—is anything but a sign of failure. Jesus was tempted, yet he was sinless! Understanding the flesh is important because it allows us to rest more easily in the presence of Jesus with the fleshly desires continuing to swirl.

Discussion

The ideas that we are discussing in this session can be very personal. It is important, as we discuss them, to come ready to be vulnerable—but also sensitive to allow others to share their own experience. We all have the flesh. None of us gets to choose this. And it is in the realm of the flesh that some of our greatest embarrassments and struggles come. So as you enter into discussion, do so with both vulnerability and humility in hearing the stories of others.

1 When you hear the word *flesh*, what comes to your mind? What images or pictures or parts of your imagination are awakened by the very word?

2 Share what you have heard in your journey regarding the flesh. What ideas or thoughts have you been given that inform what you think about this topic?

3 What aspects of your story have been most impacted by your flesh? What parts of your life continue to be given over to the realm of the flesh?

4 How do you feel sharing about the fleshly part of yourself? Does any embarrassment come along with recognizing the parts of your life where there are still uncrucified desires?

5 Have you ever asked yourself this question: "How can you still struggle with _____ after following Jesus for this long?" If so, when you hear that voice, what is its tone?

6 Finally, do you believe, on some level, that having to deal with your flesh can have a positive effect on your pursuit of Jesus? For example, has wrestling with your flesh made you a humbler person, desperate for the touch of God?

Reflection Questions

1 In this session Swoboda gives a definition of the flesh. Do you think this definition makes sense and captures the biblical understanding of the flesh? Why or why not?

2 In regard to his marriage, Swoboda thought his unwanted desires would end when he said "I do." He calls this the "myth of diminishing desire." Have you ever had similar expectations? And were those expectations met? Explain.

3 Swoboda shared elements of his own story where the flesh continues to be alive. Do you think it is easier or more difficult to follow a leader who is aware of their own areas of struggle? Explain.

4 After humanity left Eden, they did not lose their desire. Rather, their desire became unhitched from the presence of God. How and where have you seen God's good desire inside of you become corrupted?

5 One of the core ideas Swoboda discusses is Paul's command not to reform or change the flesh but to crucify it. This idea is a consistent New Testament theme. The flesh can't change; it can only be killed. What is the difference between crucifying the flesh and trying to change the flesh?

6 Practically speaking, if we are seeking to crucify the flesh, how do we do that? What can we do on a tangible level to place the flesh on the cross?

7 It can be difficult to discern the difference between a good and godly desire and an evil, sinful, fleshly desire. When you think about these two kinds of desire, what can you look at to help tell the difference? What marks a good desire? And what marks a fleshly desire?

8 Swoboda distinguishes between "longing" and "lusting" as a way to differentiate good desire from fleshly desire. Do you agree with his assessment of the two?

9 Have you ever experienced a moment in your life when you walked in victory over your flesh? If so, what can you remember about that story that gave you the strength to do so?

10 Similarly, have you ever experienced a moment in your life when you were unable to stand against the flesh and gave in? If so, what can you recall about that story that contributed to the decisions that followed?

11 When we walk into the glory of Christ upon our resurrection, we will be free of the flesh for good. Does that truth bring you hope? How does it change your outlook on the struggles you face today?

Closing

This session was perhaps more personal than some would be comfortable with, but it's important that we wade into the waters of our lives to find Christ therein. We can't change what we are unwilling to accept in the first place. We must begin with honesty and truthfulness. Over time, as we bring our true desires into the presence of the Holy Spirit, we will increasingly walk into victory. But it will take time, patience, and a great deal of grace.

WANING DESIRE

Introduction

We all lose our desire from time to time.

There may be many reasons we lose a particular desire, whether it be for love, companionship, romance, God, church, doing devotions—you name it. We might want something one day but not want it the next. Some desires wax and wane with the tides of life. Others, however, go away as a result of real, lived experience. Often desire can dissipate as the result of great hurt and pain. If, in the past, our desire has led to an experience of heartache or trauma, our own hidden survival instincts for self-preservation and self-protection against such hurt can naturally cause our desire to atrophy. If our romantic experiences only lead time and again to painful abandonment, then that part of us designed to protect ourselves can cause our desire for romance to diminish. If the church has brought about nothing but confusion and hurt, then our desire to go to church may very well dissolve. If our desire for God has led us into broken expectations and unmet hopes, we may find that our desire for him wanes.

What do we do when we face a loss of desire for God? Lenny Luchetti, in his article "Overcoming Spiritual Slump," defines this experience as a "spiritual slump." He describes it this way:

> The person in the spiritual slump experiences a diminished desire for intimacy with God through practices like prayer, Bible reading and Christian fellowship. Every disciple will, at some point, battle spiritual aridity, apathy and stagnancy. Several

so-called heroes in the Bible experienced the same. Abraham slumped into manipulative lying. Peter slumped into fearful denial. David slumped into boredom, lust, adultery and murder. The spiritual slump can happen to the best of disciples.[1]

Losing our desire for God is a painful experience, and often it comes with great shame. Many parents know this experience. We desire to be parents who show great love, care, and compassion to our children. And while we have this desire, we often find that there are times when our desire to be parents comes and goes. Or times when, for that matter, we don't want to play with our children. We want time by ourselves. When any of us experience this loss of desire, it puts us in a tedious position of being forced to do the right thing even when we don't want to. Parents often have to meet this challenge head-on. It is a mark of a good parent. But underneath this loss of desire can come a new and vexing experience of shame that I would have even momentary loss of desire. In my worst moments, when I'm not giving myself grace, I interpret this loss of desire as a sign that I'm not a good father. Self-accusation soon swoops in and gets right to work.

Part of following Jesus is being willing to learn how to respond to times when we lack a desire for him. It is not uncommon for anyone to experience a loss of desire with the people they love: children, spouses, parents, churches—even God. The human heart is a fickle organ. And it can, from time to time, experience a total loss of desire for God. Like me as a parent, if we're not careful in those vulnerable moments, we can wrongly interpret that loss of desire as some kind of shameful accusation that we don't really love God. But in reality, we are simply dealing with a fickle heart.

As an experiment, you may find it helpful to take some time to read biographies of Christian saints through history. Read a biography about Mother Teresa, Augustine, C. S. Lewis, or Martin Luther. What you find will surprise you. While we tend to exalt these heroes in our minds, we often forget the real gritty fabric of their lives. All of our saints went through far more struggle in following God than we want to believe. Many of them went through agonizing seasons wherein they lost almost their entire desire for God. St. John of the Cross put words to this plight. He called it the "dark night of the soul." Equipping ourselves with this knowledge helps us journey with Jesus over the long

---

1. Lenny Luchetti, "Overcoming Spiritual Slump," Seedbed, July 26, 2021, https://seedbed.com/the-spiritual-slump-a-new-resource-for-pastors-groups-and-individuals/.

haul. It enables us to recognize that we are not alone. People throughout history who have loved God have gone through this very vulnerable and painful experience.

But we must remember the greatest commandment: "Love the Lord your God with all your heart and with all your soul and with all your mind" (Matt. 22:37). The commandment is clear and penetrating. We are to love God above all. But nothing—not one fleck—of this commandment has anything to do with our fickle feelings at a given moment. And there is a reason. The biblical command to love is a form of love that is not dependent on a stable state of emotions. Rather, it is a covenant love that endures even when the desires and emotions come and go from our hearts. We don't only love with our desire. Sometimes we have to learn to love *through* the absence of desire. In fact, it is only through embodying the first commandment that we are able to do the second: "Love your neighbor as yourself" (Matt. 22:39). Loving God first helps us love others. Just as the character of Christian journeys to the Gates of Light without his family in Bunyan's *Pilgrim's Progress*, we must make the pilgrimage to Jesus first. Only in doing so can we come back to love our family well.

Back to parenting. I consider it one of the greatest gifts in the world to my son that he has a father who knows the difference between love and desire. He is loved, and not only when I feel like loving him. The most life-changing kind of love is the love that perseveres through the cold absence of desire.

In the Protestant world, we've done an excellent job of dismantling theologies by which we do "works" to make it to God. Sadly, I fear, in their place we've created a kind of "works of desire" whereby our righteousness is built on nothing less than our desire alone. It's dangerous to place too much weight on whether I'm desiring God today. Some days I do. Some days I don't. I know this: the overemphasis on my desire for God is not a spirituality based on God but a psychology based on the self—overfocusing on what we are doing as a way of showing how we are doing with God. Listen, no one is more interested in Christians reading their Bibles than I am. But it does seem like an odd switch. For so many, the way we show that we are good with God is to name something *we* are doing. But of course, in Christ, we have "every spiritual blessing" already (Eph. 1:3). And discipline does not determine who we are.

It is very important that we love God with our desire. But our love for God cannot be dependent upon our desire. From time to time, all of us lose touch with the true desires of our hearts. One of the most helpful ways we can begin to reconnect with our desire is to ask ourselves: Where are we most disappointed in life? How, then, could this help us get back in touch with our desire? After all, disappointment is always a wound of desire. It reveals something we wanted but never received. Taking time to reflect on our greatest disappointments always has a way of helping us discern what parts of our story we never got to fully live into. Usually, it is impossible to return to a healthy desire without coming to terms with how our desires were wounded in the first place.

G. K. Chesterton is widely believed to have said, "There are two ways to get enough; one is to accumulate more and more. The other is to desire less." Perhaps one positive outcome of experiencing a loss of desire for God is gaining a deeper appreciation for what we already do have rather than wanting and needing more.

Discussion

From time to time, we all experience a loss of desire for someone we love. And we may anticipate having the same experience in our love for God at some point. As you ponder the waning desires that come with the Godward life, consider your own experience and attempts at following Jesus. In light of your own experience, discuss the following questions with those around you.

1 For a few moments, have everyone in the group share a story of a time when they sensed a waning of their love either for a person in their life or for God.

2 After everyone has shared, take some time to reflect internally on what led to that sense of lost desire. What happened? Why do you believe your desire seemed to go away?

3 Think about your experience of lost desire from the previous two questions. Did the desire dissipate overnight? Or did it take some time for it to dissipate?

4 Finally, in that same story, did the desire ever return? If so, what were some of the steps you took to help you reconnect with that desire? If not, what steps are you currently taking or could you start taking to cultivate a renewed desire?

Reflection Questions

1 In this session Swoboda discusses some of the moments in the Bible when biblical characters appeared to have lost their entire desire to live. Why do you think these moments were included in the Bible? Why would God inspire these stories into the narrative of Scripture?

2 One of the claims Swoboda makes in the book is that we live in a moment when some people would prefer to live in a universe without a God who desires us. His claim is that desire always demands some kind of response. Do you believe this is true? Do you believe that God desires us and invites us to respond? Explain.

3 One of the core concepts in the video and the book is the relationship between desire and duty. Desire is when we *want* to do something. But duty is our way of walking when that desire is no longer present. Why is understanding duty so important for the Christian?

4 Take a few moments to reflect on a time in your life when you lost desire and had to walk through a relationship (with God or someone else) out of duty when there was no desire. Was it painful? Difficult? Or did you find it easy? Explain.

5 Leaning only on duty in a relationship can eventually lead to toxicity. Why is this the case? Why are there limits to duty?

6 Swoboda discusses the idea of "desire cultures" versus "duty cultures." At our moment in time, which one do you believe is more descriptive of your environment? Why? What contributed to that?

7 Much of our Christian worship music today says, "God, I want more of you. Give me more of you." Is it possible for God to give us more than he already has in giving Jesus, his Son? Explain.

8 Conjuring up excitement and desire for God is not listed as one of the fruits of the Spirit in the New Testament. Yet too often we have a works-based approach to Christianity that seems to imply one truly loves God only when their desire is growing. What do you think about this assessment?

9 Have you experienced what Swoboda calls "desire envy"? Have you ever felt jealousy toward others who appear on the outside to have a deeper desire for God than you do? Explain.

10 If you have experienced desire envy, how have you responded to it?

11 Do you believe everyone is supposed to love God with the same level of desire? Or are people different, and do they approach Jesus with different kinds and levels of desire?

12 Identity plays a critical role in walking through our waning desire. How and why is it so important to know our true identity when we seem to be experiencing a loss of desire?

13 What are practical steps you (or anyone) can take to begin cultivating a renewed desire for God? What have you seen that helps? What doesn't help?

Closing

In this session we examined the loss (or waning) of desire that is a normal experience for anyone in a loving relationship. The goal here has been to help you identify some of those places where you can find a vacuum of desire. Now we move forward to our next topic: undesired desire.

UNDESIRED DESIRE

Introduction

Admittedly, this may be the most dangerous session of this study. Historically speaking, discussions about desire from a Christian perspective have been littered with landmines. Oversimplification often has been our most vexing enemy. It has been easy for us to say, "Change your desire," or "Stop wanting that," expecting that all will magically turn out fine and dandy. "Just pray those desires away," some have been quick to say. Such a simplistic perspective uncritically views desire as some kind of spicket to be turned to the right or the left. But humans aren't faucets, and desire rarely works like that. In recent years, it has become increasingly evident that experiences such as reparative therapy can be extremely harmful for people who experience unwanted sexual desire. Sadly, such practices often do not take into account the complexities of human desire. The results have proven, for too many, traumatic.

Here in session 6, we explore "unwanted" or "undesired" desires—those longings within us that we wish we didn't have or experience. Though some of our desires may be intentional and chosen, this is not always the case. Not every desire in our hearts is one we want or choose. Pretty much all of us can find our hearts riddled with an array of desires, some of which produce within us great frustration and consternation—if not tremendous shame.

Part of the journey of Christian spirituality is our willingness to join with the Holy Spirit in examining these unwanted desires with a spirit of curiosity. At least this is what the apostle Paul did. At a critical juncture in Paul's writing of Romans, he confesses,

"I do not understand what I do. For what I want to do I do not do, but what I hate I do" (Rom. 7:15). Quite vulnerably, the apostle himself narrates in his letter of encouragement and instruction to the church of Rome that he walks with desires that he doesn't want to have—or at least that his action is driven by desires he wishes he didn't have. That Scripture would so boldly declare the errant desires of Paul for all of posterity should speak to our own experience. Those who have taken up the call of the Godward life can expect, from time to time, to find within themselves unwanted desires.

Often we wake up to these desires over time and by experience. I remember one particular evening a number of years ago when I was pastoring in Portland. The church had grown significantly, and I was feeling increasingly weary from the responsibility. Behind the scenes, it had been determined that we needed a shift in the church. During a leadership meeting, when our entire team was present, we began to outline some changes. Our entire focus that evening was to give sustained attention to our decision to initiate eldership in the church. Given that the church was young, we had waited to do this until we felt as though a critical mass had formed and we had some mature Christian leaders who could take this role upon themselves. And I was getting tired. I needed help. Given the needs of the church, we needed to move toward a shared leadership approach. We sang some songs in worship, prayed, and then I made the announcement. When I shared with our team that we would be shifting to shared leadership—that I was going to be doing less—the leaders in the room responded by applauding. Loudly. *Too* loudly.

Everyone was wildly pleased with the decision. After cleaning up, we all said goodbye and went home. That evening, as I lay in bed, I felt hurt. I couldn't put my finger on it. Why was I feeling so hurt after such a great evening? Then it dawned on me. All the leaders in the church applauded that I would slowly be stepping out of the way so other leaders could be established. Their applause gave voice to their desire. That experience was very important in my own maturity process. It awakened in me the realization that I have an unhealthy secret desire to be more wanted by the church than I should be.

Their applause exposed some narcissism. It revealed to me an unhealthy need to be wanted. Nobody in that room was trying to hurt my feelings. They were simply affirming the fact that our church needed a better leadership team and that nobody wanted me to burn out. Their applause was birthed in a beautiful place. But the experience uncovered in me an unhealthy desire to be more important than I ever should be. I never would have seen that had they not applauded so excitedly.

I feel almost embarrassed sharing this story. Why? Because I don't desire to have such self-centered desires. But I do have them. And I've increasingly learned that the only way they can be properly addressed is by shedding light on them. The flesh inside wants to be the center of attention, the one everyone looks to, the person who is most needed. I don't want this desire. But I have it. And part of my journey as a Christian leader is learning to embrace not being the center of attention, not wanting to be so wanted, and instead helping others enter into their God-given roles as leaders in the church.

All of us, from time to time, have moments of epiphany like this when we become aware of desires within us we wish we didn't have. Some of these desires may have to do with our relationships, our sexuality, our vocation, our jobs, and even our bodies. Many of us will wrestle with these unwanted desires for the rest of our lives. But what is most important is not that we have unwanted desires; it is what we do with those unwanted desires.

Those places in our lives where we willingly deny ourselves for the sake of following Jesus—especially in the realm of desire—are where we can mature the most. As Thomas Merton once said, "Love is not a matter of getting what you want. Quite the contrary."[1] Love, in the Christian story, is not an exercise in curating and gaining everything our hearts desire. Indeed, sometimes the most loving thing we can do is crucify our unwanted desires in the name of love.

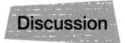

Discussion

The nature of unwanted desires can bring up many emotions for us, especially given how this conversation often overlaps with our theological beliefs about sexuality. Perhaps we even feel a sense of shame that we harbor particular desires in ourselves. Still, we don't do ourselves any favors by hiding in the darkness. Light exposes. And light can heal. Come into this discussion with a great deal of sensitivity to the other people in the room.

---

1. Thomas Merton and Naomi Burton Stone, *Love and Living* (San Diego: Harcourt Brace Jovanovich, 2002), 34.

1 As you think about unwanted desires, why do you believe we experience these desires? What does it say about our nature as humans that we have wants that we don't want?

2 Have you ever experienced an unwanted desire? If so, and if sharing it with those in your discussion group would be appropriate, what was (or is) the nature of that desire?

3 In your discussion, share how it feels to bring this unwanted desire into the light. Is it difficult? Is it liberating?

4 In your own story of walking with the desires that you find within yourself, what has been your approach to dealing with them? What has been your way of responding to these desires?

5 Discuss how you have felt or sensed shame in your life as a result of these desires.

6 Finally, together, share the hope. At this moment in your journey, where is the hope in your story?

Reflection Questions

1 What is one thing from this session that you found to be helpful?

2 What is one thing that was difficult or challenging to hear?

3 In this session Swoboda shares about "strange desires" and a woman who had a lifelong desire to eat couch cushions. As you think about this story, does it make you feel a sense of compassion? Or confusion?

4 Where do our unwanted desires come from? What from the storyline of the Bible might help us understand their origin?

5 What do you think and feel when you consider the fact that Paul experienced unwanted desires? Does it bring you hope? How? Why?

6 One of the studies spoken of in this session suggests that less than 5 percent of our daily desires are actually chosen out of the will. Do you believe this might be the case? How does this statistic change your perspective on desire?

7 Swoboda tells a story of being asked to list his heroes in the faith. All of them, he shares, have one thing in common. None of them got everything they wanted. They never fully arrived. How, in your mind, might *not* getting everything we want be a pathway to Christian maturity?

8 The book of Hebrews says, "These were all commended for their faith, yet none of them received what had been promised, since God had planned something better for us so that only together with us would they be made perfect" (Heb. 11:39–40). How does this passage speak to our current conversation about unwanted desires?

9 Have you ever had an unwanted desire go away? If so, what happened? What made this happen?

10 Swoboda says that pain can be a gift in his discussion of Jesus' healing of the lepers. Do you agree with his assessment? Why or why not?

11 In the end, can the struggle and pain of carrying unwanted desires make us deeper and more mature people?

12 After having watched the content from this session, how do you believe you should walk alongside others who experience unwanted desires?

Closing

We come to the end of session 6 and our discussion of undesired desires. I'm reminded of the words of St. Ignatius of Loyola, who said, "We should not fix our desires on health or sickness, wealth or poverty, success or failure, a long life or a short one. For everything has the potential to call forth a more loving response to our life forever with God. Our only desire and one choice should be this: I want and choose what better leads to God's deepening life in me."[2] Ignatius, above all, wanted God. This was his greatest desire. And while we may not always feel that way, it should be our goal as followers of Jesus. We all have unwanted desires. But those are not our greatest desires.

---

2. Quoted in David Fleming, *What Is Ignatian Spirituality?* (Chicago: Loyola Press, 2011), 2–3.

KILLING DESIRE

Introduction

The human heart is a complex thing. In this session we are dealing with the issue of the heart—but through a particular lens. We are asking if the human heart can be rid of sinful desires. That is, how do we "kill" desires in our heart that we know are not good and godly?

My son was about five years old when his mother and I began to have conversations with him about the discipline of generosity at the church, including the giving of one's time and money. We explored with him the idea that the life of a Christian should be marked by financial generosity toward the community. I recall one car ride home from church when Elliot piped up from the back seat, "Why am I supposed to be generous with my money, Dad?" In an attempt at parental brilliance, I told him something along the lines of, "When you give God your generosity, you enjoy the gift of being obedient." He sat there quietly. After a few moments, he confessed, "But I don't want that."

Children's gift to adults is their capacity for honest confession. They often speak the truth we are unwilling to say. What does a five-year-old have to give to the church? Well, the amount, we explained, is less important than the heart that generosity forges within us. That is, it is about the act of faithfulness, not the amount we give to the Lord. Sitting in the car, taking in this new idea, my son spoke what every adult thinks but doesn't have the guts to say. His heart offers us a little insight into all of our hearts. We are all prone toward hoarding, keeping, and withholding. Our hearts can easily become bent toward the love of things over the love of God. This is, in essence, the reality of the human heart enslaved to idols. Our hearts tend to love things over God.

In this session we touch on some of the debates that have taken place in the church. One such debate, between Augustine and Pelagius, was over the issue of whether the heart could truly be changed by its own merit and goodness. Those following Augustine's line of thought have traditionally been quite pessimistic about the state of the human heart and our ability to change it through hard work and willpower. People like John Calvin would go on to write about the heart as an "idol factory" that constantly produces altars to false loves and desires.[1] And this is true. But the human heart is also complex. History is replete with moments when the human spirit has been able to produce good things like penicillin, the First Amendment, hospitals, and heart transplant surgeries. The human heart is a dynamic and disturbing thing able to undertake great good and great evil in the same breath. Humans have the capacity to enact that which brings flourishing. But humans could also come up with the Holocaust. We are, indeed, an odd race.

I've found in my own self that the debate between Augustine and Pelagius is represented by two extremes in my spiritual life. On one hand, there are times when I struggle with desire that I simply can't change or get rid of. On the other hand, at other times I am walking in victory over my sin and my evil desires. When I'm unable to change myself, my besetting sin becomes self-hatred and loathing. But when I'm able to change and walk in victory, my besetting sin is pride and judgment of others for not being who I am. I oscillate between being Augustinian and Pelagian for a few weeks on end. Running between the twin peaks of shame and pride becomes exhausting. When my identity and security are found in how I'm doing, the whole Christian walk is an enterprise in works. Only when I recognize the grace of God when I walk in victory and the same grace when I'm overcome by a desire for sin do I find peace.

While elements of the Augustine and Pelagius debate continue to this day, one thing is not debated: the effects of sin and our desire for it on the world. Evil desire is corrosive. What begins as desire becomes action, which then impacts the world. Sin doesn't stop with my own actions. Sin goes viral. It's systemic. Ironically, those among my community of theologically conservative Christians who admit that personal sin affects all of human existence are often most resistant to the idea that systemic sins of racism, hatred, greed, and ecological harm are realities. And equally ironic is the fact that progressive Christians are likely to tackle systemic issues without calling people to

1. For a full exploration of this theme, see Richard Keyes, "The Idol Factory," in *No God but God: Breaking with the Idols of Our Age* (Chicago, IL: Moody Publishers, 1992).

holiness. If sin affects *everything* in human life, doesn't it by extension affect *everything* in human culture? Indeed. No matter how hard we try, we simply can't get the blood off our hands. Broken human desire seeps into everything we do and everywhere we go.

Because the human heart is broken, an essential part of Christian spirituality is the process of "killing" desires. Some desires need to be healed. But some simply need to be killed. I suggest three steps to confront our temptations and evil desires: confess, cut, and fill. By confess, I mean finding someone with whom we can name and give voice to the desires within. This person may be a friend, a pastor, a confidant, a family member, or a counselor. But we need a safe person with whom we can speak about the things churning within us. Then we need to practice the biblical call to "cut," as exemplified by Jesus telling his disciples to "cut off" any part of our lives that gets in the way of discipleship (Matt. 5:30). And finally, we need to fill ourselves with good desires.

With that, session 7 invites us once again to look at how we can walk faithfully with Jesus with our wayward desires.

Discussion

As you prepare to discuss this session, take a few moments to write down on a sheet of paper some of the highlights of the content that was shared. What stood out to you? What did you notice? How did your heart engage what was shared? Did you feel a sense of relief? Did you feel challenged? Now that you've spent a little time reflecting on what you absorbed in this session, take the next few minutes to discuss together the following questions.

1 In this session you heard Swoboda discuss "the heart." When you take time to assess as honestly as possible the state of your heart, what words come to mind? What are some of the immediate descriptors you would use concerning your own "guts"?

2 How do you think the human heart changes? Does it change? Or is it beyond repair?

3 If the heart can undergo change, what are ways this can happen? How have you experienced real heart change in your own life?

4 Part of the spiritual life is facing temptations that draw our hearts away from God. Jesus told his disciples to "cut off" hands and "gouge out" eyes if they cause us to stumble. What do you think Jesus meant by this?

5 What are some of the things that help you to face temptations that are part of the normal life of following Jesus?

6 Do you often "confess" your own inner desires to someone? Why or why not?

Reflection Questions

1 After watching this session, how do you think differently about the reality of the human heart?

2 Do you tend to be more pessimistic about the human heart and believe it cannot change? Or do you tend to be more optimistic about its capacity to make changes?

3 As you see it, is it possible for the human heart to undergo transformation through sheer effort? Or is something else needed?

4 An important discipline described in this session is confession to one another. In confession, we speak truthfully to God about what is going on inside our hearts. But we also share with each other what is going on inside. Which do you tend to focus on? Confession to God or to others?

5 The book of James speaks about confession as being healing to us (5:16). How, in your mind, does confession to one another bring about healing?

6 Do you think, after having watched this session, it is important for us to confess our sins to each other? Why or why not?

7 As this session described, some temptation comes from the outside and some comes from the inside. Why do you think this is the case?

8 Swoboda says that sin often snowballs. As you think about the nature of sin in your own life, would you agree with this assessment? Explain.

9 If it is true that sin snowballs, does this underscore the importance of being more honest about our struggles? Why?

10 We sometimes think confession is telling God something he doesn't know. But this is not what the Bible has in mind. How has this session changed your understanding of the nature of confession to God?

11 It is one thing to "cut" out behaviors and activities that hold us back and distract us from a Godward life. But we also need to "fill" ourselves with good things that can help bring about new life. What might this look like?

Closing

We come to the end of session 7 and our discussion about "killing desire." The last few sessions have dealt in large part with sinful or evil desires. But our trajectory takes a new direction here. We move from facing our dark desires to beginning to awaken and nurture the good and godly desires we are meant to have. The next session on "nurturing desire" will explore how we can begin to take steps to inculcate desires that bring life and flourishing. Keep up the good work!

NURTURING DESIRE

Introduction

How do we nurture good desires within ourselves?

It is easy to want things that are not good for us. Every parent knows this reality intimately. There are so many different kinds of foods available in today's marketplace. In any major city, one can find foods from every culture and ethnicity. In a grocery store, one can locate healthy and not-so-healthy foods in the same aisle. With the internet at our fingertips, we can make anything at home we wish. The variety is astounding. In that context, how does a parent help their child (at as early an age as possible) fall in love with good, healthy food in a world of empty carbs, sugars, colas, and Happy Meals? Let's be honest: for a child, what's a kale salad compared to fast-food chicken nuggets?

We are all born with evil desires and must learn how to desire rightly. Aristotle refused to believe there was even the possibility of love at first sight. First sight, he believed, only made space for one to conceive of the desire to enter into friendship with another person. Even friendship is not something that can be born in a moment's notice; it takes time. The very act of learning to love a friend involves not only our affections toward that person, but also the hard work of actually getting to know them at a level that penetrates far deeper than first impressions and first thoughts. Aristotle and the New Testament share a little bit of perspective. A good desire isn't always natural to us. But we can learn to develop good desires.

Back to food. It turns out that even our tastes around food are not fixed and immutable. We can change our desires for different foods with a little intention and discipline. A good deal has been written about how one can train a child's desire for good foods. In one particular study, published in 2015, researchers watched how children related to their food. They concluded that when a child is exposed to vegetables for about fifteen days, a new lifelong love for green foods can be established. They called this period of time the "flavor window." This research suggests that by giving sustained attention to our tastes, we can actually begin to teach our children to desire foods that are good for the body, bones, and spirit.

Our desires will not be entirely changed when we begin to follow Jesus. But lack of immediate change doesn't mean there is no hope. Rather, over time, our desires begin to be transformed as we follow Jesus. God begins to reshape our desires around the way of Jesus through the miracle of the Holy Spirit's indwelling. What is needed are time, trust, and a great deal of patience. We begin to be nurtured into the good desires that bring flourishing and life on the eternal level rather than just for the moment. Temptation always trades something in for a momentary or short-term enjoyment. It suspends our ability to see the long view. This is why the fruit of following our temptation is sorrow and death—it trades eternal flourishing for momentary flourishing. Following the Spirit's desires, on the other hand, always leads me toward decisions that bring long-term, even eternal, peace.

Take the New Testament teaching on ambition. Even our ambitions need to be sanctified. Ambition is not bad. Paul commands Christians to "eagerly desire the greater gifts" (1 Cor. 12:31). He says, "Make it your ambition to lead a quiet life" (1 Thess. 4:11). He even tells a church that it is a "noble task" to "desire" to be a leader in the church (1 Tim. 3:1). Ambition is part of God's character. Consider the scope of his desires. God's vision for the world is one where everyone would live a life of justice, goodness, mercy, and forgiveness. God desires all to know the grace of God. What an ambitious desire! As John Stackhouse wrote, "God's work is greater than any one cause. Or to put it better, God's one cause is the extension of his influence, his kingdom, into and over all the world, every corner of it. God's view is total, his resources infinite, and his ambition literally universal."[1] Ambition is rooted in God's nature. He has a universal desire for all to experience him, and he is interested in reshaping our ambitions around the character of Christ. Part of following Jesus is nurturing the right ambitions.

---

1. John G. Stackhouse, *Church: An Insider's Look at How We Do It* (Vancouver: Regent College Publishing, 2005), 170.

This truth is driven home in the New Testament, which celebrates doing good *with the right intentions*. Paul mentions the Thessalonian church's "work produced by faith, [their] labor prompted by love" (1 Thess. 1:3). He commends them for the reason and rationale behind their work. They're not just doing it. They're doing it for the right reasons. Motivation, in the Christian life, really matters. How often do we see people go into the ministry for the wrong reasons? It is entirely possible to do good with malformed intentions.

We need to have our desires nurtured. How can we do this? In this session we'll explore some of the key ways that we can be people of great intent who seek to nurture our desires around the way of Jesus. Our call is to nurture the higher desires, and a central way this happens is through the cultivation of habits that shape those desires. Our habits and our souls go hand in hand. There is an intimate relationship between our habits and the wiring of our brains. The same is true of desire: there is an intimate relationship between our habits and our desires. Some of these habits come with time and through personal experience. As Paul writes in Ephesians 5:10, "Find out what pleases the Lord."

Discussion

The topic of nurturing desires likely brings up a number of talking points that you'd be wise to discuss with those around you. The idea of actually seeing change in our desires may seem impossible, but with the gospel and the sanctifying and nurturing work of the Holy Spirit, all things are possible. Our desires can, indeed, undergo a transformation. With this in mind, discuss the following questions together.

1 As you reflect on the content of this session, what in particular stands out to you? Why do you think it stands out?

2 Swoboda talks about how we tend to nurture our desires around what we do. Do you agree with this assessment? Why or why not?

3 As you think about the nurturing of desires, what activity in particular has had a disproportionate impact on your own desires? What do you do that has (either positively or negatively) shaped what you want?

4 What do you think changes first: our desires or our actions? Explain.

5 Can you think of a moment or two over the course of your life when you experienced a changed desire? What led to it? Why did it happen?

6 If you could nurture one or two good desires within yourself today, what would they be? Why would you want to experience those desires?

Reflection Questions

1 What key disciplines or actions do you believe would be instrumental in the formation of your desires?

2 Do you think God cares about the reshaping and formation of our desires? Why or why not?

3 Is mere action all that matters? Or do you think the desire behind our action makes a difference in its validity and goodness?

4 Think through your life story. Have you ever had a moment when a desire led to harm of self or others? Reflect on the relationship between that desire and the way it brought harm to yourself or others.

5 Have you ever sought to nurture a new desire but found that you fell short of reaching your goal? Explore that story for a few minutes in reflection.

6 After having reflected on that story, what do you think got in the way of the goal of a new desire?

7 Sometimes we *want* to want something. That is, we want to have a desire for something. What is one thing that you wish you wanted?

8 Assess whether wanting this thing would be good for you.

9 We tend to think repentance is merely something we do with our lives. But a key element of repentance is the reshaping of our insides. Do you think repentance is something we can do in the realm of our desires? Can we and should we repent of certain desires? Explain.

10 Upon reflection, do you believe God is inviting you to repent of certain desires? What are they? And how important is it that you walk in obedience regarding these desires?

11 Part of nurturing good desires is having incentives in place that lead us in the right direction. How can we build into our lives incentives for the cultivation of good desires?

The aim of Christian discipleship is for us to be renewed by the Spirit of Jesus to such a degree that our desires are entirely reoriented to God. This doesn't just happen. It takes time, intentionality, and great care. In our next session, we'll look at understanding how to love the right things the right way—the *ordering* of desire.

ORDERING DESIRE

Introduction

What do we desire the most?

When it comes to our desire, we often face two big problems. The first, quite simply, is that we don't always know what we actually want. Some time ago, a financial planner explained to me that his work entailed helping people achieve their desires over the course of their lives. But he pointed out that many people have a hard time identifying what those desires actually are. He couldn't help people achieve their desires if they couldn't identify them. Perhaps because of the decision paralysis we all often feel in a world with endless pathways, many of us struggle to know what our heart's desire is.

Second, we equate our own desires with God's desire. Years ago, Susan B. Anthony reportedly said, "I distrust those people who know so well what God wants them to do, because I notice it always coincides with their own desires."[1] Anthony's point is poignant— and important. We can all be found guilty of equating our own desires with God's. Too often, we make judgments and decisions based on what we want rather than what God desires.

These two difficulties can easily create great challenges for us. In this session we'll talk about the practice of "ordering" one's desires in such a way that these problems begin to be addressed. By having a proper order to our desire—by loving the right things the most—we not only begin to identify the desires we *should* have, but also start prioritizing God's desires over our own.

---

1. Quoted in E. C. Stanton et al., *History of Woman Suffrage: 1883–1900* (New York: Fowler & Wells, 1902), 263.

Catastrophe awaits when we have disordered desires and love certain things to the wrong degree. When we have disordered desires, we don't care well for our children and don't stay attuned to their needs. We don't attend to the work God has given us to do. Our marriages and friendships begin to fall apart. Our bodies begin to break down. In my years of working to help people understand the principles of a biblical sabbath, I've discovered that more than anything, burnout is the result of disordered desires. Burnout is what happens when we love good but temporary things as if they were ultimate things. We love money, success, and the feeling of accomplishment over and against deep and nourishing relationships with people, good health, and the pursuit of the way of Jesus. This is why the sabbath is such an important principle for people who love their jobs. In all my years, I've never met someone who burned out because they hated their job. Sabbath is important for people who love their work. It keeps their work from becoming their god.

This is one of many reasons we must learn—in the effort to nurture our desires—to order particular desires over others. Not all desires are of equal value. Nor should they have equal weight in our lives. Sometimes we put too much of our sense of self into what we are doing and forget who we are. One of the healthiest things we can do is to stop leaning on all the things we are doing for God and enter into a season of being reminded who we are in God. When we walk through a season of exhaustion and find no life in keeping up with our Bible reading plan, we should stop the Bible reading plan and sit in the presence of God. Or we should put down the discipline that has run its course for a season and find, once again, the grace of God in a new way.

One of the most important places we begin the process of ordering our desires is in our conversational life with God. There are two ways we give shape to our lives. We tend to bend truth to our desires. Or we will bend our desires to the truth. If, and when, we see ourselves as the center of our lives, it becomes impossible to discern the difference between our desires and God's will. That is, I see everything I want as God's will. God bends to me. In an interview, Robert P. George—in discussing the importance of prayer—says that the danger of this kind of worldview is that it leads us to a belief that we are the center of our universe:

> Of course the real danger with any human life is rationalization—going on the basis of mere feeling. If you rely just on feeling, then most of the time you are going to think that, well, if I want to do something, then that must mean that God wants me to do it.

Why would God have put this desire in me if he did not want me to do it? So then we confuse God's will with our desires, when in fact God may be willing that we resist those desires, and it is our temptation to rationalize them, to do what we want to do, to do what we feel like doing, what would seem to give us pleasure and give us something that we want—power, status, prestige, or what have you. And then we rationalize it by claiming that this is what God wants or means us to have so that we could do more good.[2]

The call to Christ is not merely to do good. Rather, it is to be formed into the kind of people who do good supernaturally as a result of the Spirit's transformative power. Altruism without transformation is not salvific. This is why Judas Iscariot could be inspired by a demon as he claimed to care about the poor. Ill intentions ruled his heart. Dallas Willard prophetically understood this tension, writing,

> The general human failing is to want what is right and important, but at the same time not to commit to the kind of life that will produce the action we know to be right and the condition we want to enjoy. This is the feature of human character that explains why the road to hell is paved with good intentions. We intend what is right, but we avoid the life that would make it reality.[3]

Discussion

In this session we are talking about the task of "ordering" our desires—seeking to clearly identify and orient our lives around the right desires. These are the highest desires, the highest ideals, the most important things God lays before us. Not the good things, but the "best" things—to borrow from Paul (Phil. 1:10). As we think about these things, consider the following guiding questions for your discussion.

---

2. Robert P. George and Kevin Spinale, "Attend to Your Spiritual Life," Robert P. George, July 12, 2016, https://robertpgeorge.com/articles/attend-to-your-spiritual-life/.

3. Dallas Willard, *Spirit of the Disciplines* (San Francisco: Harper and Row, 1988), 6.

1 As you've done in a couple of the other sessions, take time to identify some of the things that were said in this session that stood out to you. Why did they stand out?

2 In your group, take a few moments to share about some of the core and guiding desires of your life. Name them with as much specificity as you can.

3 As you think about these desires, would you say they reflect God's desires? Or do some of the driving desires within you fail to connect with the way of Jesus?

4 What do you think are the top five most important desires God has for you? Or for any person? Why do you think that?

5 In your group, share one desire you give far too much attention, time, and resources to please or satisfy.

Reflection Questions

1 As people who seek the way of Jesus, how can we identify the most important desires? Where do we ground our knowledge of these desires?

2 This session deals with the issue of prioritization—of putting certain desires over others. How important is it to prioritize certain desires to have healthy relationships and a flourishing life?

3 In this session Swoboda discusses the biblical theme of jealousy, how God is jealous but we are told not to be jealous. What do you make of this? And how does it speak to our understanding of the prioritization of our desires?

4 One of the core concepts in this session is "mimetic desire," the idea that certain desires are shaped within us because we see them in others. How do you believe relationships can shape and order our desires for the positive?

5 And how can relationships shape and order our desires for the negative?

6 Bernard of Clairvaux is famous in Christian history for his idea of the "degrees of love." How, in your mind, does this concept correlate to our conversation about the ordering of desire?

7 Based on what you give your time, energy, and resources to, what would you say you love the most in your life?

8 Does this thing reflect what you *want* to desire the most? Or are your ideals and your real lived experience at odds with each other?

9 One of the ways Jesus discusses an ordered love is through the concept of hating. First, does Jesus' idea of hating correlate with what our cultural moment believes about hate?

10 Second, how does Jesus' invitation to hate actually help us see the ordering of our own loves?

11 Based on this discussion, do you think God hates? If so, how?

12 What discipline can you begin to practice to help you reconfigure your desires to be rightly ordered? What can you do to step toward ordering your desires in a good and godly way?

As we noted earlier, the sessions we are now walking through deal less with dark or evil desires; instead, we're exploring how the Spirit of God helps us arrange and orient our desires in a way that reflects God's desire. Now we move toward the relationship between our desire and the future. God made humans as people who "long."

RESURRECTING DESIRE

Introduction

In this session we see how desire fell off the biblical landscape following Genesis 4. Something in the realm of desire led to the fall of humanity. So for nearly the rest of the Bible, there is little discussion about it.

Desires can hurt us. Expectations can make or break us. If we expect our lives to be filled with ease and endless joy, we will likely experience great disappointment in due course. The higher our expectations—or desires—for the way things will turn out, the more we set ourselves up to be hurt. If we expect that we will no longer have any struggles after we get married, we put ourselves in a position to experience tremendous heartache. Just as expectations can hurt us, so can desires that are connected to the wrong things. If we pursue a desire ardently but never actually achieve that desire, we may decide our existence isn't worth living.

This session discusses the intimate relationship between pain and desire. Often we are most hurt by people who use our desires against us. For many, the hurt our desires bring upon us can lead to a complete loss of desire. We find living a life *without* desire to cause us significantly less pain than living a life of unfulfilled desire. This is why those who have been abused report that the abuse they experienced—on some level—met some need and even brought a semblance of pleasure. The guilt that comes alongside this realization can often be too heavy to carry. For too many, myself included, sexual abuse provided something the soul longed for. The act was evil. But it provided something that was deeply needed: a caress, attention, being wanted, being chosen. For a moment, in a world where I felt unseen and unwanted, *someone* saw me and wanted me. And in the abuse, a need was met. Then came the shame that the abuse brought some joy or pleasure or arousal. Such shame can lead to self-hatred. If we don't stop to grieve and process, desire itself is shamed and cursed as though it were a bad thing that leads to bad places. We end up killing our own desire so we will never be in a position to be hurt that way again.

There is a physical dimension to reactions like this. Psychologists and neuroscientists discuss how, when someone is touched and caressed, the body is flooded with oxytocin and dopamine, neural chemicals that create bonds and the sense of pleasure. The experience of being touched in a sexual way can be euphoric, even in the context of abuse. Those who have been abused may come to feel a tremendous sadness that their abuser was the first person who seemed to see them and want them. In fact, victims often report that their abuser "knew them better than anyone else." Thus, an abused person should never be shamed for naming the sense that something in their abuse brought them fleeting life. Rather than being cursed, those desires that were met should be blessed. Indeed, we were made to be wanted, to be seen, to be loved, to be held. Groomers almost always find something their targets desperately want and seek to fulfill it. They know their prey. They study their victims closely, going out of their way to understand and make it known that they understand.

But the biblical story doesn't put a premium on getting everything we think should be coming to us. Rather, the Bible holds up the virtue of thirsting, of hungering. This, in and of itself, is an act worth blessing, and indeed there is a blessing for the thirsty desire one has for God. In that same vein, throughout Scripture, to be empty is often cast as a virtue. For instance, in 2 Kings 4, a woman has a conversation with Elisha. He asks her what she has, and she says all she has is a little oil. Elisha tells her to go and get a bunch of empty jars from the neighbors and then pour oil into the empty jars. The oil stops only when there are no more empty jars.

What does this story show? It is a beautiful story because it speaks to God's desire to fill empty things. God's filling comes not to those who are already full; God fills the empty, who have the capacity to be filled.

Part of our task as followers of Jesus is to open ourselves up to a constant hunger and thirst for God, even if we never seem to receive what we believe faith should produce. This is the "resurrection of desire," the awakening of desire toward God in this life.

Discussion

For your discussion time, turn toward the people you are with and prepare to reflect on the following questions together.

1 What stood out to you from the video session that you think is worth mentioning?

2 Can you identify a time in your life when you experienced great wounding or pain as a result of your desire? What happened? How did your desire bring about pain?

3 In light of that story, how did you relate to desire afterward? Did you enter again into desire? Or did you run away from desire in an effort to protect yourself?

4 From your vantage point, what is the greatest "wound of desire" you have ever faced?

5 What, more than anything, has awakened your desire for God and God's desires for your life?

Reflection Questions

1 In this session Swoboda discusses how the biblical tradition engages with the Hebrew word *t'shuqah* (translated "desire" in the NIV). What do you make of this?

2 How do you think the first humans responded to the fall? Do you think they walked through shame and self-hatred? What happened next?

3 And, similarly, what happens to you after you fall? Do you notice anything regarding your own desire?

4 Swoboda discusses how often we turn toward "non-desire" to protect ourselves from further hurt. Do you agree with this assessment? Have you ever seen this play out in your own life? Explain.

5 When someone becomes a Christian, what do you think begins to happen to their desire?

6 This session touches on the topic of desire for the life to come. Do you believe we will experience desire in heaven? And if so, what does that say about human beings?

7 Swoboda points to the way desire is spoken of in the Song of Songs. There appears to be a renewal of the desire that was lost after Genesis 4. How does desire get restored? What is taking place?

8 Can you think of a time in your life when you thought it would be better if you didn't desire at all? Why did that thought cross your mind?

9 Thirst and hunger play important roles in this session and are equally important in the biblical tradition. How does the Bible describe thirsting and hungering?

10 How do you think our desire will be different in the presence of God than it is right now?

Closing

In this session we looked into how God gives new life to our desire when we are in Christ. We begin to enter into God's design for our desire, and we begin to awaken to a desire for our future with Christ. Now we turn to our final topic—the "longing desire" God has put into each of us for the future and our ultimate reconciliation with God.

LONGING DESIRE

Introduction

I remember early in my faith asking what the word *Bible* meant. You wouldn't guess the real answer listening to Christian clichés. I was told the word *Bible* stood for "Basic Instructions Before Leaving Earth." Upon years of reflection, I've come to find that nothing could be further from the truth. The Bible is anything but basic. There is far more story than instruction. And the final two chapters of the story don't depict us leaving this earth and going to heaven but heaven coming to us and invading earth. The goal of the Christian life isn't leaving, escaping, or abandoning. The goal is living rightly here on earth, under God's rule and being. Christianity isn't about detachment. It's about living in our true humanity. Here and now. Desire and all.

When Christians think about the future, they have the habit of doing so in a disembodied way. We fail to pay close attention to core texts in the Bible like Revelation 20–22 that invite us to see the future in very earthly terms. Heaven will be here on earth. When we think about heaven, we must not see it as an escape from earth. Quite the opposite. Heaven is going to be heaven and earth once again married and one—forever.

Humans are made to long for something.

In this session we explore one part of the creation story that often goes unexplored. As we discussed in session 2, humans are the one creature in the created order made with the capacity for longing. That is to say, they were made to have hearts and minds that long for a life with God forever. This is why our secular culture tends to be so obsessed with things like zombie apocalypse and dystopian fantasies. In a world that no longer grounds itself in the knowledge of God, it must have some kind of future hope or orientation. Our obsession with eschatology (the study of the end times) in cinema and television reflects that longing—albeit one devoid of God. We were made not only to long for the future. We were made to long for a future with God.

One way the Bible speaks to this truth is through the story of "faces." Although humans were made to be in a face-to-face relationship with God in the garden, that intimacy has been lost. But not forever. As the apostle Paul writes in 1 Corinthians 13:12, we will once again see God face-to-face. This is what should (and does) sustain the human soul. Our hearts long for a day when all that was lost after Genesis 3 will be restored to its intent. And all desire will, once more, be oriented toward all that is right and good.

Over the course of the last few years, I've lived in the Pacific Northwest. One of the values of a place like Oregon is that a high priority is given to justice in our urban environments. This prioritization of justice is a gift, but it can pose some difficulties. People often feel a kind of justice exhaustion, not knowing what stuff they are obliged to be angry about this week.

Nonetheless, there is a longing, a cry of the heart, for the world to be one of justice. What is perplexing about this is that in the Pacific Northwest, where people long for justice on so many levels, religion plays an increasingly diminished role. Fewer and fewer people identify as Christians and connect to local church life.

Yet our streets, newspapers, and cultural landscape pulsate with a longing for the world to be made right.

This longing for a brighter future is an innate human condition. Without something to hope for, we lose our sense of meaning, value, and purpose. We were made to orient toward a future day when all will be made right, evil will be undone, and the tears will be wiped from our eyes.

Scripture names the longing of the heart of every human being in the world.

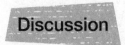

Discussion

We have taken space to explore the ways in which we long for a glorious future. Everyone—religious or not—is made with an innate desire to see the world become something good and just. Doesn't this longing speak to having been created with a heart for the future? In this final session, take some time to discuss the following questions as they relate to the video.

1 What is the human heart's greatest longing?

2 What happens when we seek to fulfill the human heart's greatest longing with other things?

3 When you think about heaven, what is your greatest desire?

4 Do you believe humans will have desire when we are with God in the new creation? If so, what will be different about our desire? And what will be the same?

5 Why do you think God gave us a built-in longing in the first place?

Reflection Questions

1 In the video for this session, what is one thing that stuck out to you?

2 Why do you think so many people today are obsessed with zombie apocalypse and dystopian novels? What makes us love these stories so much?

3 One of the key ideas Swoboda brings up in the discussion is how both heaven and hell are places of desire. What is different between the two of them?

4 God's wrath is described in very interesting terms around desire. What is that desire? And what do you make of this?

5 God builds delay into our lives. Adam experienced it as he waited for the woman. And we too experience it as we await the return of Jesus. What does God accomplish in the process of delay?

6 In your life, how have you benefited from waiting for something that you really wanted?

7 Does getting everything we want actually fulfill us—does it deepen us as people? Or can it end up harming us and stifling our growth?

8 Sum up, as best you can, what this session says about the face of God.

9 Near the end of the session, Swoboda describes the conversion of Count Zinzendorf. What strikes you about this story?

10 Why do you think Zinzendorf became a Christian after seeing the thorns on Jesus?

11 The title of this study is *The Gift of Thorns*. Having undergone this journey, can you see how thorns can indeed be a gift to us?

12 As you conclude this journey, what is one lasting thought that will remain with you?

Closing

What a gift it has been to walk this journey with you. You have invested time and hard work into the process. Kudos! And while our journey through *The Gift of Thorns* is coming to a close, the pathway forward stretches on. As we continue to follow Jesus into a future that seems scary at times, we have hope. And we can look forward to the glorious day when our desires will be healed, made new, and restored to their original design. Let's close with another prayer:

Thank you, Lord God. Thanks for making us as desiring creatures. And thanks for loving us enough to meet us in our desires. Heal us, Lord. And return to us very, very soon. Maranatha! Come, Lord Jesus!

The Gift of Thorns

Jesus, the Flesh, and the War for Our Wants

A. J. Swoboda

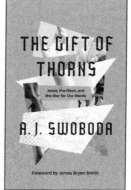

There's a War Being Fought Over Our Wants

Our desires and longings are being weaponized against us by cultural, spiritual, and relational forces. "Follow your heart" and "You do you" have become our moment's mantras. Yet too many in the Christian community assume desire is in and of itself bad and dangerous and must be crucified.

Some demonize desire. Others deify it. The result for too many is feeling torn asunder by the raging desires within.

What do we do with our wants? What about our unwanted wants? And how do we cultivate desires that bring life and freedom and lead to Christ? To answer these questions and more, *The Gift of Thorns*, by A. J. Swoboda, dives deep into Scripture to learn about human desire, Satan's desire, and even God's desire.

What makes a follower of Christ is not whether we have desires but what we do with them. And when we discover God's good will for our wants, we'll find that the things we thought were thorns may in fact be the greatest of gifts.

Available wherever books are sold.